My
★ Grandpa's ★
War

WRITTEN BY David Volk

ILLUSTRATED BY Jason Folkerts

To Luca –
Hope you enjoyed the
4th grade.

Sincerely!
[signature]
4-27-13

To Rick

My appreciation to Rick Eilert who was a great help with this book. Rick served in the Marine Corps in Vietnam and the grandpa character in this book was modeled on Rick's experiences in Vietnam and his long struggle with the injuries he received there. Tragically, Rick recently died of a heart attack. He was a loving husband, father, a true patriot and my dear friend. I will miss him very much. Rick loved his Marine Corps and their motto best sums up how he lived his life:

SEMPER FIDELIS (Always Faithful)

INTRODUCTION

My name is Mae. I am 9 years old and I want to share a story with you. There are no wizards or vampires or other magical characters in this story, but there is one special person: my grandpa.

I know, I know—everyone's grandparents are special. They love to spoil us. They even put bumper stickers on their cars that say things like: "If I Had Known Grandkids Were So Great, I Would Have Had Them First!" But something happened to my grandpa, and recently he became even more special to me. So this is our story, his and mine.

First off, let me tell you that while my name is Mae, Grandpa calls me Sarge. He gave me this nickname because of a very close friend he served with in the Vietnam War. His friend's name was Sergeant May. Also, I am a bit of a tomboy, and Sarge is a good nickname for a tomboy.

My grandpa and I like to share things. Ever since I can remember, we have gone for pancakes every Saturday morning at our local diner. Often we meet some of his buddies there. Many of them are veterans like my grandpa. That means they've been in the armed services, like the army. I like them a lot. They always tease me-*Especially when Grandpa calls me Sarge.*

CHAPTER I

My grandfather grew up in a small town and lived a small-town life. Later, he went away to college, where he met my grandma. They both planned on becoming teachers. However, one day my grandpa got an official letter in the mail. That letter changed everything for them. He was being drafted into the U.S. Army! I never really knew what being drafted meant. Now I know. I always thought soldiers just volunteered, but back during the time of the Vietnam War, young men were drafted. That meant they were just told to report for military duty. They had no choice.

Not long ago, I decided to study up on the Vietnam draft. I learned that some young men went to Canada so they wouldn't be drafted. In Canada they couldn't be arrested for avoiding the draft, which was illegal in U.S. I asked Grandpa what he thought about that. He paused a little bit before he answered. He was thinking hard, and then he said, "Sarge, this country has been very good to me and our family, and sometimes debts come due that have to be paid." I think Grandpa was telling me that when someone or something has been good to you, and also those you love, that you have a duty to repay that debt.

After going off to something called basic training to learn how to be a soldier, Grandpa was sent to another army post and trained to be a corpsman. He told me a corpsman was also called a medic, sort of like a doctor. Medics were people who would go into combat with other soldiers. If someone got hurt, the medics would take care of him until he could get to a hospital. Grandpa told me he was always glad he became a medic because he liked the idea of possibly saving a life in war instead of taking one.

And that's how he got his nickname. All of his army buddies call him Doc. I never knew that before.

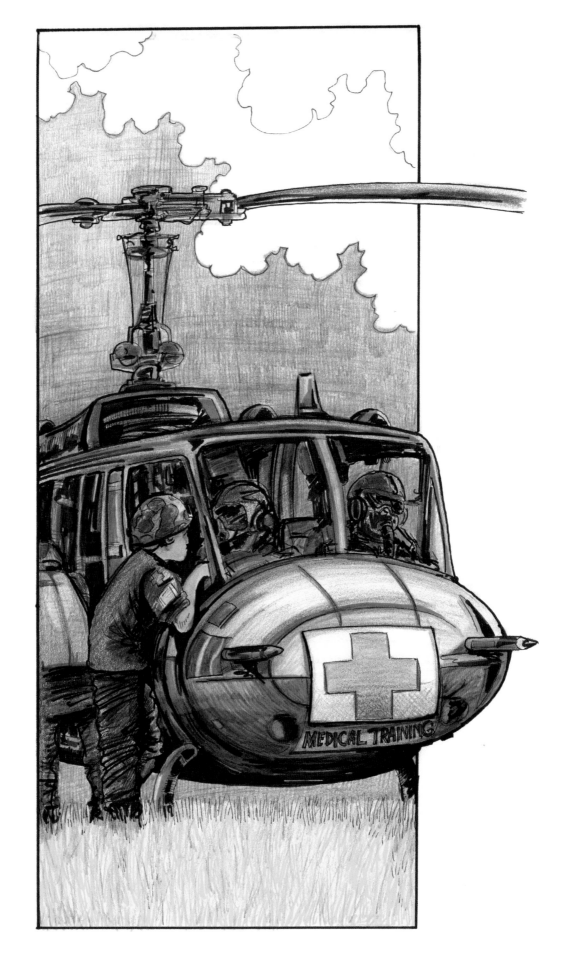

CHAPTER II

Coming from a small town in the Midwest, Grandpa said going to the army was a strange experience. He never talked about the bad things that happened to him when he was sent to Vietnam after his training. I know he served with a unit called the 101st Airborne Division. He has a drawer full of medals, so he must have done a good job being a soldier.

But I kept asking him to tell me more. So one time he explained it this way: "Sarge, what's our favorite movie?" I answered *"The Wizard of Oz,"* the one we watch together every year. "Well," he said, "I kind of felt a lot like Dorothy; one day I was a young guy hanging out in our comfortable little town, and the next minute I was plopped down in a very different kind of place called Vietnam. However, unlike Oz this place was very real and a jungle that could be very scary.

He said that the jungle was every shade of green imaginable, and thick with plants and trees and vines, which actually made it dark, even in the daylight. It was so very different from the prairie where he had grown up. He also said it had **"lions and tigers and bears, oh my,"** which got me laughing as he was quoting *"The Wizard of Oz."*

Grandpa said Vietnam was especially bad during the monsoon season when it rained for days and days at a time. He and the other soldiers would get soaking wet and stay that way for weeks. The bugs were another horrible part of the jungle and the monsoons. He said there  were mosquitoes so big they could carry off small children. Grandpa likes to exaggerate sometimes. I think this was one of those times.

He also told me about some of the good things he did in his job as a medic. One story makes him smile every time he tells me. He was in a remote village, taking care of some of the sick people, when he learned there was a woman about to have a baby. He went to where she lived, a house made out of bamboo with a thatched roof. Since he had the most medical training, he delivered that baby right there.

He told the Vietnamese family his name and where to find him in case they needed help later. He got to know that family very well because he went back several times to treat the baby for some bad infections.

"Sarge, I was more nervous delivering that baby than anything else I did in Vietnam," he would always say with a shake of his head.

This year I did a school report on the Vietnam War. I have to admit it is a difficult thing to understand and then explain. I learned that while my grandpa was over there serving his country and fighting the war, a lot of people back here at home were protesting against the war. Sometimes not in very nice ways and there was even some violence.

I saw a picture once in a magazine of a protest march. The protesters were carrying the flag of our enemies. I just couldn't understand how they could do that. I asked Grandpa about it, and he said, "Well, Sarge, when you live in a country like America, people have the right to do things that you don't understand or might not agree with. That was a difficult time for our country." I still don't understand it, but if it was okay with Grandpa, it was okay with me.

CHAPTER III

I mentioned that my grandpa has a drawer full of medals. One of them is called the Purple Heart. It is given to American soldiers who are wounded during a war. I also mentioned that something happened recently that made me want to write his story.

See, my grandpa's leg was hurt badly during the war. He stepped on a land mine, which is something put into the ground that explodes if you step on it. Even though he had very good medical treatment, his injured leg never healed right. He has been in pain ever since the war, forty years ago. He's even had to have many operations on that leg. After his operations, I would always go to the hospital and read to him from our favorite books.

However, my grandpa recently lost his fight to save his leg. The doctor had to amputate it. That means to take it off in an operation.

This time when I went to the hospital afterward, I was too scared to go into his room. I was afraid something else bad might happen to him and was afraid that he would be sad.

As I stood in the doorway peeking into his hospital room and trying to hold back my tears, he finally looked over and said, "Sarge, why in the world are you looking so gloomy? Come here."

I ran over to him, buried my head into his shoulder, and started crying. After a minute, he said, "Honey, I am going to be fine, and even with my new leg I am still going to be the best dancer at the American Legion on Saturday night!" The American Legion is a place where veterans go to dance, eat, and be together.

Then he said, "Now stop crying. I have something I want to give to you." With that, he reached over on his nightstand and picked up a medal that had a bronze star attached to a ribbon.

As he pinned it on me, he said, "To Sarge, for bravery above and beyond the call of duty, and for coming to the aid of a fellow soldier, I proudly present to you the Bronze Star."

Well, of course that got me crying all over again, but this time they were happy tears.

CHAPTER IV

My grandpa is all better now and we are back to going for pancakes on Saturday mornings and watching *"The Wizard of Oz"*. We also took a special trip to our nation's capital, Washington, DC, this spring.

While we were there, we visited the Vietnam War Memorial, which is called "The Wall" because it is a huge black granite wall. It has the names of all the men and women who died during that war, including my grandpa's army buddy, Sergeant May, the soldier I was named after. You see, he died in that war. I put my hand on Sergeant May's name, which is carved in the granite with the thousands of names of other soldiers who died. I then walked off and let my grandpa have some time alone.

Today is the Fourth of the July, and it is a beautiful day. Soon, my grandpa will march by in the parade with some of his fellow veterans. Even though he has lots of friends, he is especially close to his Vietnam veteran buddies. He likes marching in these parades. For some reason, there weren't a lot parades for him to march in when he came home from Vietnam.

My grandpa is okay, and that is all that matters. He finally comes marching by, limping a little but walking proudly. All around me, people clap and cheer. My grandpa just grins. I am wearing my medal he gave me. I hold up my sign that I made the night before. It says: *"My Grandpa, My Hero!"* He looks over and gives me a smile, a thumbs-up, and then a salute, and I see him mouth the words, "Thanks, Sarge." I'm smiling so hard my face hurts! I don't pretend to understand war except that it seems to bring a lot of sadness and tragedy. The same was true of Vietnam. I also think too many people have tried to forget Vietnam and I don't think we should. It was not only my grandpa's war, but it was also the war for millions of other Americans. They deserve to be remembered and have their stories told.

Recently, my grandpa had a very special and wonderful thing happen to him. He got a letter from a man who is 41 years old and a doctor in a place called Ho Chi Minh City in Vietnam. His name is Lee Van Trahn. The U.S. Army helped him find my grandfather after all these years.

The letter said how much he and the other people from his village appreciated the work Grandpa had done for them. Dr. Van Trahn especially wanted to thank my grandpa for helping his mother. She was the woman who gave birth all those years ago. He was the baby my grandpa had delivered!

I cannot remember when I have seen my grandpa smile so much. He even contacted Lee Van Trahn. They actually hope to meet someday. I guess sometimes good things can come from bad things.

Oh, and by the way, my grandpa still is the best dancer at the American Legion on Saturday night. Just ask my grandma!

VIETNAM WAR

Map of Vietnam

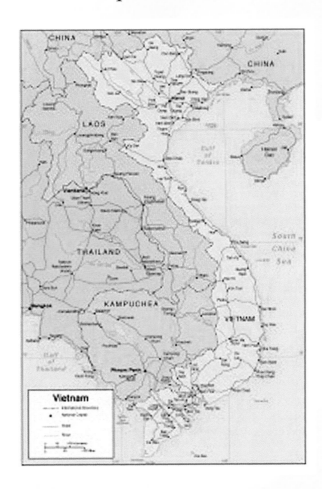

The Vietnam War was probably the most controversial and divisive foreign war in our nation's history. Even when it officially began is in question, as President Eisenhower sent military advisers to Vietnam as early as 1955, and two of those American advisers were killed in 1959.

However, one thing is certain: the war would spark conflict in America throughout most of the 1960s and 1970s. It was also the first "media war," and television would bring the war into the living rooms of Americans on a nightly basis.

Large anti-war protests were common throughout the late '60s and early '70s with over 300,000 people participating in a rally in Washington, DC, in 1971. Most of these protests took place on college campuses, where the military draft was especially unpopular. In addition to burning their draft cards as a show of protest, a lot of young men fled the country to avoid the draft. It is estimated over 30,000 American men went to Canada. They could not legally return to the United States until June of 1977, when President Jimmy Carter pardoned them.

Over 9 million military personnel served on active duty during the Vietnam era (1965–1975); over 58,000 died and 300,000 were wounded during the war. Draftees accounted for over 30 percent of combat deaths, and the average age for Vietnam vets was 19.

Although there was much turmoil and misunderstanding regarding the Vietnam War, most of the veterans of that conflict, like Sarge's Grandpa, came home and went on to lead productive, normal lives, proud to have served their country during a difficult time.

The war officially ended on April 29, 1975, when the last Americans were evacuated by helicopter from Saigon.

ACKNOWLEDGEMENTS:

Everyone who has ever written a book knows how important good friends are in helping you tell your tale. This has always been especially true with my books.

First, I would like to thank Elizabeth Squire, who gave me the idea for this book and whose husband Richard was a medic in Vietnam and who passed away a few years ago.

So thanks much to Marshall, Stephanie, Kim, Tammy, Sabrina and Mrs. Desaulniers' Fourth Grade class of Tea, SD. Also, I want to thank my illustrator, Jason Folkerts, who took a 'leap of faith' with me on this book and whose beautiful pictures tell the story of "My Grandpa's War" so well. Special appreciation to my brother Craig, the real writer in the family, who has been such a great help with my five books.

Last, but certainly not least, I wish to thank the millions of American men and women who through the years have served this country in the military. From the first patriots who picked up a musket back in 1776 to the brave young people today who have gone forward to honorably "pay debts that sometimes come due."

11694108R00021

Made in the USA
Charleston, SC
14 March 2012